Used Audio
NOSOL GLAM-KAMOR. PWALM2I
(2)

HANDLING LANGUAGE

JOHN DAVIS

BOOK 1

**Illustration ideas by John Davis
and drawn by Graham Humphreys**

D0244270

Hutchinson

London   Melbourne   Sydney   Auckland   Johannesburg

Hutchinson & Co. (Publishers) Ltd

An imprint of the Hutchinson Publishing Group

17-21 Conway Street, London W1P 5HL

Hutchinson Group (Australia) Pty Ltd
30-32 Cremorne Street, Richmond South, Victoria 3121
PO Box 151, Broadway, New South Wales 2007

Hutchinson Group (NZ) Ltd
32-34 View Road, PO Box 40-086, Glenfield, Auckland 10

Hutchinson Group (SA) (Pty) Ltd
PO Box 337, Bergvlei 2012, South Africa

First published 1981
Reprinted 1982
© John Davis 1981

Designed and produced by Logos Design

Printed and bound in Great Britain by
Ebenezer Baylis & Son Ltd, The Trinity Press, Worcester and London

British Cataloguing in Publication Data

Davis, John
Handling language.
1
1.English language — Grammar — 1950 —
1.Title
428.2 PE 1112

ISBN 0 09 143281 2

To my grandson,
Simon Jonathan

CONTENTS

THE COMMON NOUN

Every object you see around you, the table, the chair, the window, is called a **noun** in English grammar.

If it is a *common* object, without a special name of its own, like that cat shown above, it is called a common noun.

1 In this picture of an open-air bus there are many common nouns you can pick out.

driver	passenger	men	women
boy	girl	wheels	rails	dust
number-plate	hats	faces	hands

There are others you may have missed because they cannot be *seen*.

They can, however, be noticed by the senses of hearing, touch and smell, and are still common nouns:

(a) noise (to be heard from the engine)
(b) conversation (between the passengers)
(c) fumes (to be smelt from the exhaust)
(d) vibration (to be felt from the seats)

2 Make a list of common nouns, one for each letter of the alphabet. For example:
a...alligator   b...banana   c...cottage

3 Look at the picture below and write down every common noun you can see.

4 Write out the following, putting a line under each of the common nouns. There are ten to be found.

I was woken by the rain. I looked up and saw the jungle all around me. Then I remembered the plane, the storm and the crash. But all that remained was my seat from the aircraft. Apart from the sound of frogs and insects, I was alone.

5 Complete the following sentences with a suitable common noun. For example:
The footballer scored a _____ (goal).

(a) The soldier was given a _____.
(b) She sang a lullaby to her _____.
(c) I saw a good film at the _____.
(d) The mouse could smell _____.
(e) The musician played a _____.
(f) The bird picked up the _____.

THE PROPER NOUN

A proper noun is the name given to a particular person or place. To show it is a special name, it is written with a capital letter. In the picture above there are several proper nouns, for example: Tower Bridge, Victoria (the name of the ship), and the River Thames.

1   Write down the following proper nouns.
(a) five boys' names
(b) five girls' names
(c) the names of five books
(d) the names of five capital cities

2   Write out the following, beginning each proper noun with a capital letter.

My favourite uncle, uncle george, took me on a visit to london last saturday. We went on the underground to baker street station, from where it was a short walk to madame tussaud's museum. I liked best the chamber of horrors, but was quite interested in seeing what the kings and queens looked like, particularly richard the lionheart. We went into the planetarium, which was next door, and were amazed at the views of the night sky showing mars, venus and mercury. After lunch we went for a walk by the side of the river thames to have a look at the houses of parliament, and to visit westminster abbey which contains the tomb of the unknown warrior. After tea at the royalty restaurant, we took a taxi to victoria station and went home.

3   You will notice that some nouns can be either common nouns or proper nouns.

They become proper nouns when they become one particular name, spelt with a capital letter, for example: uncle and Uncle George.

Make a list of all the common nouns in exercise 2 which only become proper nouns when spelt with a capital letter.

4   Here is a list of ten common nouns:
zoo   castle   tower   loch   pier
hills   tunnel   caves   cathedral
university

Here is a list of ten proper nouns:
Blackpool   Southend   Oxford
Whipsnade   Cheddar   Mersey
Edinburgh   Coventry   Chiltern
Ness

Make a list, matching each common noun with its correct proper noun, so that *both* words become proper nouns, for example:

common noun − wall   } Hadrian's Wall
proper noun − Hadrian

The proper noun is the property of one particular name.

SINGULAR AND PLURAL

Singular comes from the word *single* and means one on its own. Plural means more than just one.

Just one dog = singular noun
= dog

More than one dog = plural noun
= dogs

The usual way of changing the singular to the plural is to add the letter -s, for example:

school + s = schools
classroom + s = classrooms

If the singular noun ends in -s, -x, -sh or -ch, you must add -es to form the plural, because without the help of the letter -e in -es, you would not be able to hear the sound of the final -s.

BUS + ES = BUSES
BOX + ES = BOXES
BRUSH + ES = BRUSHES
RANCH + ES = RANCHES

(a) Write out the plural of the following nouns.

1 animal
2 watch
3 branch
4 bush
5 nephew
6 match
7 radish
8 couch
9 moss
10 witch
11 glass
12 wish
13 mattress
14 theatre
15 sausage
16 address

(b) Write out the singular of the following nouns.

1 artists
2 writers
3 patches
4 pictures
5 vases
6 shades
7 sashes
8 churches
9 gases
10 scratches
11 foxes
12 stitches
13 houses
14 taxes
15 dresses
16 nieces

(c) Write out the following sentences, changing every singular noun to plural.

1 The rabbit runs away from the dog.
2 The girl wears a blue dress.
3 I keep the bird in a cage.
4 The priest spoke to the prince.
5 The reporter spoke to the princess.
6 The waitress served the tycoon.
7 The actress carries a bag.
8 The ship struck the rock.
9 The glass had a scratch.
10 The lioness has a cub.

The plural of nouns which end with -y

If a singular noun ends in -y, look at the letter before the -y; if it is a *consonant,* change the -y to -ies in order to form the plural, for example:

If the letter before the -y is a *vowel,* just add -s as usual, for example:

(a)   Write out the plural of the following nouns ending in -y.

1 fly	13 abbey
2 day	14 library
3 daisy	15 quay
4 alley	16 melody
5 story	17 galley
6 berry	18 lorry
7 diary	19 donkey
8 dairy	20 salary
9 chimney	21 monastery
10 storey	22 monkey
11 family	23 quarry
12 journey	24 holiday

The plural of nouns which end with -o

If a singular noun ends in -o, look at the letter before the -o to make the plural; if it is a *consonant,* add the two letters -es, for example:

There are a few exceptions to this rule, for example: piano — pianos, solo — solos, halo — halos.

If the letter before the -o is a *vowel,* just add the letter -s, for example:

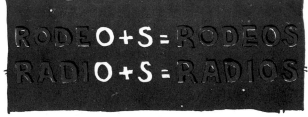

(b)   Write out the plural of these words.

1 cargo	8 shampoo
2 stereo	9 motto
3 studio	10 potato
4 patio	11 tomato
5 cameo	12 volcano
6 negro	13 tornado
7 buffalo	14 mosquito

MORE UNUSUAL PLURALS

To form the plural, not all nouns end in -s or -es; here are some different plurals.

1 If the singular noun ends in -f, change it to -v before adding -es to form the plural, for example:

wolf – wolves

Also, if the singular noun ends in -fe, the plural changes to -ves, for example:

wife – wives   life – lives
knife – knives

Write out the plural of the following words.

1 loaf	5 shelf
2 leaf	6 thief
3 calf	7 ourself
4 half	8 yourself

There are some exceptions to this rule, for example:

chief – chiefs   belief – beliefs
dwarf – dwarfs   roof – roofs

2 The names of some animals are the same for both singular and plural, as in the word sheep, for example:

Singular I found one of the sheep.
Plural The dog rounded up all the sheep.

(a) Write ten sentences (one using the word in the singular and one in the plural) for each of the following animals:

salmon   grouse   trout   cod   deer

(b) Some nouns can only ever be plural, for example:

1 clothes	6 pincers
2 trousers	7 pliers
3 scissors	8 athletics
4 shears	9 mathematics
5 tongs	10 politics

Can you think of any more?

3 There are a few nouns that completely change their spelling in the plural, for example:

man – m(*change the* a *to* e)n = men

The following nouns are in the singular. Write a sentence using each one, but with the noun in the plural.

1 foot	4 mouse
2 tooth	5 woman
3 goose	6 gentleman

Special note: child – children

COLLECTIVE NOUNS

A collective noun is a singular noun which groups together plural objects. For example: the drawing shows a flock of sheep in a pen.
A flock (*singular*) of animals (*plural*).

(a) Here is a list of collective nouns. In the spaces, put suitable plural nouns.

1 an army of _____
2 a team of _____
3 a choir of _____
4 a crew of _____
5 a menagerie of _____
6 an orchard of _____
7 a convoy of _____
8 a library of _____
9 a swarm of _____
10 a bouquet of _____

(b) These collective nouns could refer to a number of different plural nouns. Think up several for each collective noun.

1 pack   3 bundle   5 group
2 bunch   4 gang   6 set

(c) Think of collective nouns to go with each of the following groups.

1 a _____ of ships
2 a _____ of cows
3 a _____ of whales
4 a _____ of puppies
5 a _____ of pupils
6 a _____ of lions
7 a _____ of shoppers
8 a _____ of aeroplanes
9 a _____ of soldiers
10 a _____ of furniture

FEMININE ENDINGS

There are some nouns which change in form when people want to point out whether the person or animal is male or female, for example:
lion − lioness   host − hostess

Sometimes there is a slight change in the spelling before -ess is added:
tiger − tigress   actor − actress

Many nouns are completely different in the masculine and feminine, for example:
fox − vixen   brother − sister

ABSTRACT NOUNS

> **Abstract nouns are the names for all the feelings, thoughts and ideas which you cannot hear, touch or see, but which can exist in your mind.**

The difference between a common noun and an abstract noun may be seen from the following:

The *sharpness* (abstract noun) of the *knife* (common noun) made him cut his finger.

You are able to see and touch the *knife,* but *sharpness* is an idea you think of which doesn't have an actual shape.

There are several ways in which a word may be changed into an abstract noun, for example:

1 putting -ness on the end
clever + ness — cleverness
happy + ness = happiness

Note that when adding -ness to a word ending in the letter -y, you must cross off the -y and change it to an -i.

2 putting -hood on the end
child + hood = childhood
father + hood = fatherhood

3 putting -ship on the end
owner + ship = ownership
fellow + ship = fellowship

(a) Change the following words into abstract nouns, by adding -ness.

1 short
2 sad
3 rough
4 sleepy
5 crafty
6 kind
7 smooth
8 tidy
9 clean
10 weary

IDEAS
OPINIONS
BELIEFS THOUGHTS
NOTIONS

The statue 'The Thinker' is a proper noun; the words 'coming out of his head' are all abstract nouns.

(b) Change the following words into abstract nouns by adding whichever ending is correct.

1 champion
2 scholar
3 parent
4 apprentice
5 showman
6 leader
7 knight
8 man
9 priest
10 lively

(c) Change the following words into abstract nouns by changing the end of the word, or by putting the appropriate ending on the word. Some of the endings will be different from those mentioned so far.

1 honest
2 coward
3 shrink
4 patriot
5 jealous
6 difficult
7 hero
8 bond
9 serve
10 intelligent

(d) Complete the following by adding an abstract noun.

1 The thief was accused of _____.
2 A hero is known for his _____.
3 Foxes are known for their _____.
4 Dormice are known for their _____.
5 Inside the cave, all was _____.
6 The diamond ring blazed with great _____.

THE ADJECTIVE

> **Adjectives** are describing words which give nouns a fuller or more exact meaning.

For example:

The ageing film-star waved his crippled hand to the pretty reporter.

Without adjectives, this sentence would read:

The film-star waved his hand to the reporter.

We might then imagine quite a different scene. Adjectives tell your audience more about the nouns you use.

1 There is a well-known poem which tried to stop cruelty to animals; here are four lines from the poem, *without* the adjectives:

…for tigers,
And dogs and bears,
And ponies,
And hares.

Here are the lines *with* adjectives:
…for tamed and shabby tigers
And dancing dogs and bears,
And wretched, blind, pit ponies,
And little, hunted hares.

What extra meaning does the poem now have?

2 Write out the following verse, putting a line under the eleven adjectives.

Augustus was a chubby lad;
Fat ruddy cheeks Augustus had;
And everybody saw with joy
The plum and hearty, healthy boy.
He ate and drank as he was told,
And never let his soup get cold. *continued*

But one day, one cold wintry day,
He screamed out in a horrid way,
'I'll have no nasty soup today!'

3 Adjectives usually go in front of the nouns they describe, but to add variety and make phrases more interesting, they sometimes go after the noun, for example:
And did those feet in ancient time
Walk upon England's mountains green?

The adjective *ancient* goes before the noun *time,* but *green* follows the noun *mountains.*
This is more often done in poetry.

4 Write out the following piece from 'The House that Jack Built', putting a line under the five adjectives that *follow* nouns.

That waked the priest all shaven and shorn,
That married the man all tattered and torn,
That kissed the maiden all forlorn,
That milked the cow with the crumpled horn…

5 Here are the names of five animals:

lion   whale   mouse
elephant   vulture

Write some lines about these animals using a few suitable descriptive adjectives.

POWERFUL ADJECTIVES

The following paragraph about the start of our planet paints an imaginary picture which seems to be real because of the many powerful adjectives used.

(a)   The sky glows with a light, strange and dull, that of the beginning of the world. In space is a ball, the Earth, lit by an enormous oval sun, its light an intense electric blue. On Earth, lightning flashes and spurting flames light up the vivid scene; waterspouts swirl, and we can see a struggle, fierce and gigantic, between the fires and waters of our young planet. Earth is swept and covered by scalding, seething seas, on which the storms whip up tremendous waves. In the turbulent waters appear brilliant craters that spew out flames and showers of red-hot ashes that rain down into the bubbling, boiling oceans.

Here is the same paragraph but without adjectives; the facts are the same but it does not create the same picture. It is rather like comparing colour television with black-and-white television.

(b)   The sky glows with a light, that of the beginning of the world. In space is a ball, the Earth, lit by a sun. On Earth, flashes and flames light up the scene; waterspouts swirl, and we can see a struggle between the fires and waters of our planet. Earth is swept and covered by seas, on which the storms whip up waves. In the waters appear craters that spew out flames and showers of ashes that rain down into the oceans.

1   Make a list of twenty adjectives you can find in paragraph (a).

2   Make a list of ten adjectives (not appearing on this page) that you think are powerful enough to form a strong picture in the mind.

3   Write ten sentences of your own, using the following adjectives:

amazing	tremendous	splendid
fantastic	powerful	superb
stupendous	ghastly	priceless
breathtaking		

Use each adjective once only, and make the subject of the sentence suitable for the powerful adjectives.

COMPARATIVE AND SUPERLATIVE

THIS MARROW IS LARGER THAN THAT MARROW

THIS MARROW IS THE LARGEST OF ALL

1st PRIZE FOR LARGEST MARROW

The comparative adjective compares one thing with another, for example: larger, greener.

To form the comparative with short adjectives, add -er, for example:

long − longer   short − shorter

For long words, use the word more in front of the adjective, for example:

beautiful − more beautiful
intelligent − more intelligent

COMPARE MORE

(a)   Write out the following adjectives in the comparative form by adding -er or putting the word more in front.

1	hard	11	impressive
2	small	12	different
3	loud	13	educational
4	cool	14	interesting
5	kind	15	popular
6	smooth	16	effective
7	few	17	obliging
8	fresh	18	evil
9	strict	19	helpful
10	relaxed	20	important

(b)   Now choose six of the adjectives and write full sentences using each one in the comparative form.

The superlative adjective compares one thing with all the others, for example: largest, greenest.

For short adjectives, add -est to the end of the words, for example:
long − longest   short − shortest

For long words use the word most in front of the adjective, for example:
beautiful − most beautiful
intelligent − most intelligent

MOST STANDS OUT

(c)   Write out the twenty adjectives in the list opposite in the superlative form by adding -est or putting the word most in front.

(d)   Now write full sentences using six of the adjectives in the superlative form.

SPELLING COMPARATIVES AND SUPERLATIVES

'SHORT' VOWELS

1 *Short vowels* have a 'squeezed in' sound, for example: fat, hot, thin

If you wish to add the comparative -er or the superlative -est to an adjective which has a short vowel, you must *double the last letter* to make sure that the vowel keeps the short sound, for example:

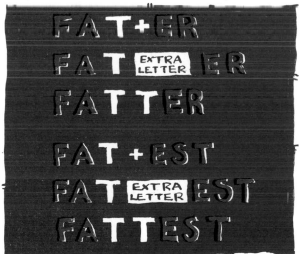

2 Adjectives with a *short vowel* followed by *two* consonants do not need an extra letter because they already have one, for example:
soft − softer − softest

Only double the last letter if there is only one consonant after a short vowel.

3 *Long vowels* have a 'stretched out' sound, for example: pale, nice, slow, clean

To add -er or -est to an adjective with a long vowel (or two vowels making a long sound) no extra letter is wanted, for example:

slow + er *or* est = slower   slowest
clean + er *or* est = cleaner   cleanest

4 If the long vowel is formed by an -e on the end of the word, you just add -r *or* -st (no extra letter wanted), for example:

pale + r = paler
pale + st = palest

nice + r = nicer
nice + st = nicest

'LONG' VOWELS

5 Write out the following sentences giving the correct form of the adjective in brackets.

(a) He is the (sad) person I know.
(b) The man became (thin) as he grew older.
(c) It was the (long) journey I had made.
(d) Yesterday was the (hot) day this year.
(e) Anne is definitely the (big) of the two girls.

ADJECTIVES ENDING IN -Y

For adjectives which end in the letter -y, change the -y to -i before adding the comparative and superlative endings.

LETTERS READY TO USE

LETTERS TO BE ALTERED

HAPPY-HAPP✸-HAPPI-HAPPIER
HAPPY-HAPP✸-HAPPI-HAPPIEST

1 Write out the comparative and superlative forms of the following words, setting out your answers like this:

Comparative	*Superlative*
shinier	shiniest

1	dry	11	weary
2	tiny	12	worthy
3	dainty	13	wealthy
4	merry	14	lively
5	crafty	15	lovely
6	jolly	16	angry
7	silly	17	clumsy
8	heavy	18	easy
9	hearty	19	tasty
10	nasty	20	weighty

2 Revision: Write out the comparative and superlative forms of the following words, setting out your answers like this:

Comparative	*Superlative*
milder	mildest

1	steep	11	calm
2	gentle	12	tough
3	black	13	blue
4	bright	14	white
5	brief	15	small
6	true	16	quiet
7	cold	17	clear
8	grey	18	sad
9	great	19	short
10	fierce	20	vague

GOOD, BAD, LITTLE, MUCH

GOOD → BETTER → BEST
BAD → WORSE → WORST

Some adjectives don't follow the common rules for comparative and superlative. You just have to learn their different forms.

(a)   Write out the following sentences, putting good, better, best, bad, worse or worst in the spaces.

1 The doctor said that both her eyes were _____ but the right eye was _____ than the other one.
2 The teacher said that my handwriting is _____ than yours, and I thought yours was the _____ in class.
3 Both tennis racquets were _____ but being a good sportsman, he gave me the _____ of the two.
4 The weather today is _____ than yesterday, but we can't expect the _____ weather to last much longer.
5 My poem is the _____ in the class and I was told it was much _____ than anything I had written before.

(b)   Write out the following sentences, putting much, more, most, little, less or least inside the blank spaces.

1 A small car costs _____ to run, as it uses only a _____ petrol to get to the town-centre.
2 This worn-out racquet is not _____ use, to say the _____, and should be replaced.
3 I wish these small children would play _____ quietly and make _____ noise.
4 As there is only a _____ lemonade left you may have it, as you have had the _____ to drink.
5 You have done _____ work than John, but Mary has produced the _____ in the whole group, and it is of a _____ better standard.

LITTLE → LESS LEAST
MUCH → MORE MOST

THE VERB

A **verb** is an *action word.*
For example:
The teacher *holds* the board.
The swimmer *dives* into the pool.

(a)   Look at the pictures above of the sporting figures and write out the following sentences, putting a line under each verb. Here is an example:
The swimmer *dives* into the pool.

1 The hockey player strikes the ball.
2 The footballer kicks the ball toward the goal.
3 The boxer in the ring punches his opponent.
4 The archer shoots an arrow at the distant target.
5 The weight-lifter lifts up the heavy weights.
6 The fencer thrusts her sword forward swiftly.
7 The golfer swings her golf-club at the ball.
8 The basketball player leaps up at the net.

9 The tennis player returns a fast ball over the net.
10 The skater glides gracefully on one leg.
11 The horsewoman encourages her horse to clear the fence.
12 The runner sprints forward in the 100 metres race.

(b)   Make up ten sentences of your own to describe the actions in other sporting activities, and underline the **verbs** you use.

(c)   In the picture above, the teacher *holds* the board at the **present** time; the action is happening now. If it had happened in the **past**, you would say that the teacher *held* the board. If it is going to happen in the **future**, you would say that the teacher *will hold* the board.

The *time* of a verb is known as its **tense**, so that we have the **present tense**, the **past tense** and the **future tense** of a verb.

Add verbs to these nouns in each of the tenses, for example:
birds *sing, sang, will sing*

1 lions _____   6 pianists _____
2 bees _____   7 jockeys _____
3 cows _____   8 elephants _____
4 artists _____   9 rivers _____
5 authors _____   10 thunder _____

THE 'HELPING' VERB

'**What I do for the verb is: supply a special service!**'

Some verbs are made up of more than one word, for example:

was helping
is holding
should be singing

The extra words, in red, are called helping verbs, or auxiliary verbs, because they help the main verb.

(a)   Write out the following sentences, putting auxiliary verbs in the blank spaces.

1 We _____ told to get on with our work and all _____ working at once.
2 At your age you _____ capable of knowing the work you _____ expected to do by yourself.
3 If Mary and Jane _____ asked to collect up the books, they _____ stacked away in no time.

The auxiliary verb helps verbs to be put in different tenses. For example:

        present
I walk, I am walking

        past
I walked, I was walking, I have walked

        future
I shall walk, I shall be walking

Here is a list of the most common auxiliary verbs:

am	was	do	have
is	were	does	has
are		did	had

shall	could	must
will	should	might
can	would	may

(b)   Write out the following sentences, putting an auxiliary verb in each blank space. There are often several possibilities.

1 Now the two dogs _____ barking fiercely at each other.
2 The little children _____ gone out to play on the swings.
3 What's the problem? I _____ be able to help you.
4 I _____ finish my homework after I _____ swallowed my tea.
5 When I _____ finished my work, I _____ help you with yours.
6 You _____ taken my book away and I _____ like it returned.
7 If she _____ forgotten to post my letter I _____ be very cross.
8 She _____ buy only one dress as she _____ not have enough money to buy a second dress.

Now say which tense each of the verbs is in, present, past or future.

VERBS ENDING IN -ED OR -ING

Put in an extra letter!

1 The usual way to make the past tense of a verb is to add the letters -ed. But in most cases, the verb has to be altered before -ed is placed on the end.

(a) To put -ed on the end of a verb with a *short* vowel (turn back to vowels on page 11) you must *double the last letter,* for example:

(b) To put -ed on the end of a verb with a *long* vowel or a double consonant, no extra letter is wanted, for example:
play + ed = played
climb + ed = climbed

(c) If the verb ends with the letter -e, you simply add -d, for example:
hope + d = hoped

(d) Change the following verbs into the past tense by adding -ed.

1 shop	11 lean
2 share	12 knit
3 skate	13 skid
4 skin	14 pull
5 stay	15 wet
6 gum	16 step
7 trap	17 fill
8 kick	18 beg
9 clap	19 enjoy
10 chat	20 excite

2 You use the form *putting* as either the present tense (am putting), past tense (was putting) or future tense (will be putting). It suggests a *continuous* action.

(a) To put -ing on the end of a verb with a short vowel, you must *double the last letter,* for example:

(b) To put -ing on the end of a verb with a *long* vowel, or a double consonant, no extra letter is wanted, for example:
clean + ing = cleaning

(c) If the verb ends with the letter -e cross off the -e first, for example:
hope (cross off the -e) = hop
hop + ing = hoping
This avoids a double vowel.

(d) Add the ending -ing to the following.

1 plot	4 cook	7 crack
2 sign	5 pull	8 stew
3 win	6 fill	9 bank

(e) Add the ending -ing to these verbs.

1 write	8 picture
2 freeze	9 move
3 retire	10 excite
4 wake	11 reverse
5 crease	12 lose
6 deserve	13 admire
7 refuse	14 purchase

VERBS ENDING IN -Y

"GET RID OF THE Y" IED

To form the past tense from a verb ending with the letter -y, cross off the -y, put the letter -i in its place and add the letters -ed.

CARRY - CARR✴ -

CARRI = CARRIED

(a) Change the following verbs into the past tense.

1 try	9 worry
2 spy	10 remedy
3 pity	11 marry
4 copy	12 apply
5 rely	13 notify
6 busy	14 hurry
7 reply	15 satisfy
8 study	16 purify

To form the present tense for he, she or it, from a verb ending with the letter -y, put the letter -i in its place and add the letters -es.

CARRY - CARR✴ -

CARRI = CARRIES

(b) Change these verbs to the present tense for he, she or it.

1 cry	9 testify
2 occupy	10 mutiny
3 justify	11 accompany
4 vary	12 satisfy
5 simplify	13 falsify
6 classify	14 horrify
7 certify	15 prophesy
8 liquefy	16 electrify

To add -ing to a verb ending in the letter -y, simply add -ing.

CARRY - CARRY +

ING = CARRYING

(c) Change these verbs to the correct form ending in -ing.

1 enjoy	3 deny	5 tidy
2 rely	4 steady	6 buy

To form the past tense with a verb which has a vowel before the -y, simply add -ed.

STRAY + ED = STRAYED

(d) Change the following to the past tense.

1 journey	5 destroy
2 betray	6 convey
3 delay	7 annoy
4 obey	8 survey

Exceptions: say   pay   lay
past tense = said   paid   laid

SINGULAR AND PLURAL VERBS

A verb is singular or plural depending on the number of people doing the actions, that is, whether the subject is singular or plural. If the subject of the sentence is in the singular the verb is also singular: if the subject is plural (or there is more than one noun) the verb is plural.

(a) The following subjects and verbs are singular; change them both to plural, for example:

singular   The dog barks.
plural   The dogs bark.

1 A mouse likes cheese.
2 The girl walks home.
3 The man sweeps the road.
4 The car drives smoothly.
5 The rabbit tries to escape from the pair of hungry foxes.
6 The rabbit is trying to escape.

If there is a 'helping' or auxiliary verb, as in the last example, this also has to be plural if the subject of the sentence is plural.

(b) In the following story, the little girl uses the wrong verbs. Write down the answers she should have given.

A little girl opened the door to her teacher.
'Hello, are your parents in?' asked the teacher.

'They was in,' said the little girl, 'but they is out now.'
'They *was* in! They *is* out!' exclaimed the teacher. 'Where is your grammar?'
'In the front room watching telly.'

(c) Write out the following sentences, putting the words was, were, wasn't and weren't in the appropriate spaces.

1 Our trainer thought I _____ good, but the others _____ hopeless.
2 They refused to go on with the training as they _____ tired and _____ getting enough rest.
3 He _____ very angry and told them he _____ prepared to put up with such poor team spirit. He said we _____ going to win the competition unless everybody _____ prepared to make the effort. It took me some time, but I _____ able to convince the others that he _____ being unfair or unreasonable.

SAW BY ITSELF ALONE

The word saw is used on its own:

I saw, he saw, she saw, we saw, you saw and they saw.
It is a *complete verb,* in the past tense.

SEEN MUST HAVE AN EXTRA VERB

The word seen is only a *part of a verb,* and in front of it must be put an auxiliary verb:

I *have* seen, he *has* seen, she *has* seen, we *have* seen, you *have* seen, they *have* seen, or they *have been* seen, etc.

(a)   Write out the following, putting just one word, saw or seen, inside the blank spaces.

1 Mary and I _____ that picture at the Majestic, last week.
2 Both of us had _____ it long before you _____ it.
3 I _____ you at the disco, and you were also _____ by Mary.
4 Elizabeth _____ us before we had _____ her.

DID USED BY ITSELF

The word did is used on its own:
I did, she did, he did, we did, you did and they did.
It is a *complete verb* in the past tense.

DONE MUST HAVE AN EXTRA VERB

The word done is only a part of a verb, and in front of it must be put an auxiliary verb. For example:
It *was* done, it *will be* done, I *have* done, he *has* done, she *had* done, they *have* done, etc.

(b)   Write out the following sentences, putting just one word, did or done, in the spaces.

1 The girl _____ the work all by herself and _____ a good job.
2 After she had _____ the work, she went to her friend's house.
3 She _____ it as quickly as she could, and has _____ it very well.
4 I think I have _____ better in this test than I _____ in the last.

HE, SHE, IT DOESN'T

I, WE, YOU, THEY DON'T

(c)   These are the negative forms of the verb to do, in the present tense. Write out the following putting don't or doesn't in the blank spaces.

1 Any girl who _____ want to play may go to the library to study.
2 She _____ think much of the idea and he _____ either.
3 You _____ have to agree with me and she _____ have to speak.
4 I shall tell her it _____ matter and that you _____ mind.

CHANGING THE TENSE OF THE VERB

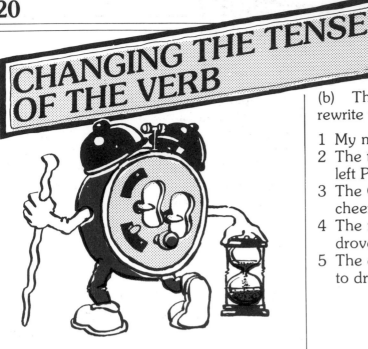

(a)   The following sentences are in the present tense; rewrite them in the past tense. (See page 14 again, if you have forgotten about tenses.)

1 My baby brother cries all night.
2 John swims for the school team.
3 Ann quietly reads her magazine.
4 I feel sick because I eat too much.
5 My parents tell me off whenever I come home late at night.
6 The library stays open until 5 p.m. on Saturday.
7 My dog barks loudly at the gate when he sees a cat across the road.
8 Jones plays for Bolton Wanderers.

(b)   The following are in the past tense; rewrite them in the present.

1 My mates went to the local disco.
2 The train bound for Manchester has just left Platform Four.
3 The Queen visited the town and cheerfully waved to the people.
4 The mechanic repaired the car and drove it out of the garage.
5 The driving-instructor taught my brother to drive his new car.

(c)   The following are in the future tense; rewrite them in the present.

1 My mates will go to the disco.
2 The train bound for Manchester will leave from Platform Four.
3 The Queen will visit the town and cheerfully wave to the people.
4 The mechanic will repair the car before he can drive it out of the garage.
5 The driving-instructor will teach my brother to drive his new car.
6 I shall just go outside for a while, to get some fresh air.
7 When we get indoors I shall play you one of my favourite records.
8 When I get some money, I shall buy records of my favourite group.

CHANGING PAST TENSE INTO PRESENT

(a)   The following story is in the past tense. Write it out again changing to the present tense; the first paragraph has been supplied, as an example.

A certain pianist *had* a theory that music *soothed* the wildest of animals. To prove it, he *trekked* to the middle of the African jungle, taking his piano with him. All round *were* the roars and screams of ferocious animals.

When he started to play, the roars died down and a strange hush fell on the jungle. One by one the animals came out to listen, sitting quietly in a circle. Suddenly, with an ear-splitting roar, a lion leapt from the jungle and bit off the pianist's head. The other animals were shocked and aghast.

'You idiot!' trumpeted the elephant. 'Our one chance of hearing beautiful music gone for ever. Why did you do it?'

'Eh?' said the lion, cupping a paw to his ear. 'What did you say?'

Example: first paragraph
A certain pianist *has* a theory that music *soothes* the wildest of animals. To prove it he *treks* to the middle of the African jungle, taking his piano with him. All round *are* the roars and screams of ferocious animals.

What is the different effect of the present tense?
Now continue the passage.

(b)   Rewrite the following passage as though you were actually there, giving a reporter's eye-witness account. Not *all* the verbs should go into the present tense, you will find.

The power of the English long-bowmen had pushed back the French armies. It seemed certain that unless a miracle happened, France would be utterly defeated.

A peasant girl, Joan of Arc, made her way to the castle where the Dauphin, heir to the French throne, had his court. She claimed she had seen visions and had a call from God to restore the Dauphin to power. Of course the courtiers scoffed, until Joan unhesitatingly recognized the Dauphin where he stood carefully disguised among them to test her. The Dauphin believed she had been given divine powers, and told her that she would now take supreme command of the French forces.

NOUNS THAT CHANGE PLACES WITH VERBS

VERB

ALSO A NOUN

There are many words which look the same, but may be used either as a noun or as a verb.

Often the noun stresses the first part of the word, for example: *refuse* (noun) which means something worthless, left over after use; the verb stresses the second part of the word, for example: *refuse* (verb) which means that you will not accept, or will not give in to something.

(a)   Write out the following sentences, putting noun or verb in the spaces. For example:
The men said that unless they got more pay they would refuse (verb) to cart away the refuse (noun) to the town depot.

1 The centre-forward hoped for a transfer (....) to Sunderland but his manager refused to transfer (....) him.
2 A jury cannot convict (....) a man accused of a crime, simply because he has already been a convict (....).
3 The police arrested a rebel (....) who said that even if he were to be put in prison he would still rebel (....).

4 The student wanted to research (....) the movement of frogs' legs, but couldn't get any money for her research (....).

(b)   Make up thirty sentences of your own using the following words. The sentences should be in fifteen pairs, the first sentence using the word as a noun, and the second using it as a verb. Sometimes their meanings are quite different. For example:
The pioneers found a *spring* in the hills and filled up their barrels.
The lion hid in the bushes, ready to *spring* on the unwary buffalo.

1 bowl
2 suit
3 rock
4 ring
5 iron
6 watch
7 model
8 wave
9 lock
10 drink
11 judge
12 strike
13 shadow
14 hammer
15 produce

(c)   This time two nouns are used in a different sense.
    Prisoner: 'You're locking me up? What's the *charge*?'
    Policeman: 'There's no *charge*. It's all part of the service.'

PERSONAL PRONOUNS

> Pro- means 'instead of'.
> A pronoun is a word that is used *instead of* a noun.

Personal pronouns used for *one* person are:

| I | me | you | he | him | she |

her   it

When used for *more* than one person:

we   us   you   they   them

For example, some pronouns in use:
Mary gave *me* a book and *I* gave *her* a fountain pen.

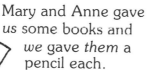

Mary and Anne gave *us* some books and *we* gave *them* a pencil each.

(a)   Write out the following, putting suitable pronouns in the blank spaces.

A long-haired lad walked into a barber's shop.

'Give _____ a Tom Jones haircut,' _____ demanded.

The barber gave _____ a short back and sides.

'Tom Jones doesn't have his hair cut like that!' the lad shouted.

'_____ does when _____ comes here,' was the reply.

When to use those and them:

It is important not to confuse these two words.

Use those before a noun, because it is an adjective. For example:

those people   those animals
those plants   those objects

Them is a personal pronoun and is used *instead* of a noun. For example:
I like them *But* I like those records.

(b)   Write out the following, choosing them or those.

1 I have read _____ books before and I would like to read _____ again.
2 _____ girls are my friends and I go out with _____ to dances and parties.
3 'I prefer _____ gloves,' said the girl, 'and I will take _____ in the dark-brown colour.'

THE ADVERB

ADVERBS

Adverbs give more meaning to the *verb* by saying how, when or where the action happens.

There are three main kinds of adverbs:

(a) The adverb of *manner* which tells you how an action is done. For example:
badly   well   quickly
eagerly   slowly

1 The athlete ran (verb) quickly (adverb).
2 The tortoise crawled (verb) slowly (adverb).
3 The boy hurt (verb) his hand badly (adverb).
4 The artist painted (verb) well (adverb).
5 The girl eagerly (adverb) attended (verb) the youth club.

(b) The adverb of *time* which tells you when an action is done. For example:
now   then   soon
before   since   yesterday

1 Yesterday (adverb) I lost (verb) my fountain-pen.
2 She had already finished (verb) her work before (adverb).

(c) The adverb of *place* which tells you where an action is done. For example:

1 I can't find (verb) the books anywhere (adverb).
2 I have looked (verb) for her everywhere (adverb).

Most adverbs are made by adding -ly to an adjective, for example:
quick − quickly   wise − wisely

If the word ends with the letter -l as in beautiful, make sure that this letter is kept in the word as well as the new -l in -ly; this will mean that there will be a double-l, as in the following:
hopeful − hopefully
beautiful − beautifully

GRACEFUL + LY = GRACEFULLY

If the word ends with the letter -y as in pretty, replace the -y with the letter -i before adding -ly, as in the following:

busy − bus* − busi + ly = busily
crazy − craz* − crazi + ly = crazily

HAPPY - HAPP* HAPP = HAPPILY

Turn the following adjectives into adverbs:
heavy   weary   faithful   thoughtful
bestial   cranky   grand   low

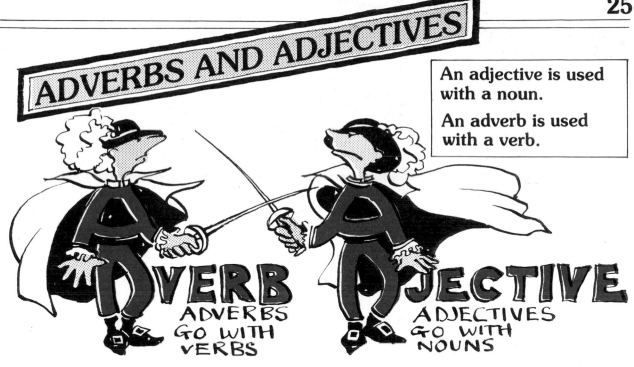

ADVERBS AND ADJECTIVES

ADVERBS GO WITH VERBS

ADJECTIVES GO WITH NOUNS

> An adjective is used with a noun.
>
> An adverb is used with a verb.

(a) Write out the following, putting adjective or adverb in the spaces, for example:

She thinks she is good, but in fact is a very bad (adjective) player.

She thinks she is good, but in fact she plays very badly (adverb).

1 She apologized and said it had been an accidental (....) mistake.
   She apologized and said that she had done it accidentally (....).
2 You may rely on her; she keeps regularly (....) to her time-table.
   You may rely on her as she keeps a regular (....) time-table.
3 I am hopeless at maths and can't work these out correctly (....).
   I am hopeless at maths and can't provide a correct (....) answer.
4 Why do you keep on speaking to me so angrily (....)?
   Why do you keep on speaking to me in such an angry (....) way?
5 With a quick (....) jump, the brown fox was over the lazy dog.
   The brown fox jumped quickly (....) over the lazy dog.

(b) Write out the following sentences, choosing a suitable adverb or an adjective from the pairs of words in the brackets.

1 She plays netball (poor, poorly) but I play (good, well).
2 Write this composition out again more (careful, carefully), and this time take the trouble to write more (slow, slowly).
3 The teacher spoke (sharp, sharply) to the girl because she had handed in homework which had been done (untidy, untidily).
4 She danced as (beautiful, beautifully) as a ballerina, and when the dance was over, she curtsied (graceful, gracefully).
5 You should not be acting so (scornful, scornfully) just because he speaks clearly and (distinct, distinctly).
6 Please act (sensible, sensibly) and everything will work out (good, well).
7 It's good to see her so (happy, happily) after getting such (brilliant, brilliantly) results.
8 The clown was (busy, busily) mixing another bucket of whitewash with a (gleeful, gleefully) look in his eye.

THE FULL STOP

A sentence should make full and complete sense. It begins with a capital letter and ends with a full stop.

There are times when a sentence has made complete sense and needs to come to a halt with a full stop, but in error a *comma* is used instead, and what should be two sentences are pushed together as one. This can often happen when a *noun* is followed by one of the *personal pronouns* (see page 23).

For example: My father came down to make his breakfast (noun), he (personal pronoun) is usually in a hurry in the morning.

Correction: My father came down to make his breakfast. He is usually in a hurry in the morning.

(a)   The following have been printed as sentences, but in fact there should be a full stop between a noun and a pronoun. Rewrite each one as two separate sentences.

1 I sometimes take my dog into the park, it loves to run free.
2 I have a dog and a cat, they get on very well together.
3 You were told to hold on to his collar, you just don't seem to like animals.
4 Our dog shows great intelligence, we teach him many tricks.
5 My cat likes to eat fish, her cat will only eat tinned meat.

6 My little sister wanted a puppy for her birthday, she had to be content with a stuffed dog that squeaked.
7 An aunt of mine has three cats, I much prefer dogs.

Two sentences are often also written incorrectly as one when a *noun* is followed by another *noun* which has no connection with the first one.

For example: My father came down to make his breakfast (noun), mother (another noun with no connection) told him to hurry or he would be late.

Correction: My father came down to make his breakfast. Mother told him to hurry or he would be late.

(b)   Rewrite each one of the following as two separate sentences.

1 Mary sat down to play the piano Robert left the room.
2 The dog hid under the table the cat followed Robert.
3 Mother came into our room the noise had woken her up.
4 Mary again sat down to play the piano she played even louder.
5 The dog hid under the table that animal hates loud noises.

FULL STOP EXERCISES

1 Three full stops are needed to make sense of the answer to the following joke. Write it out so that the reader would understand it.

Defendant: As God is my judge, I do not owe the money.

Judge: He isn't I am you do pay up.

2 You will notice that four full stops have been missed out of this notice of netball regulations. Write them out correctly.

Netball is a seven-a-side team game, usually played by girls as in basketball, points are scored by sending the ball through a ring at the opponents' end of the court players may pass the ball by throwing it, but must not run with it they have to keep inside certain areas of the court

3 The printer has missed out seven full stops in the following story. Rewrite it correctly.

A lion was walking through the jungle when he came across a deer eating grass in a clearing the lion roared, 'Who is King of the Jungle?'

The deer replied, 'Oh, you are, master.'

The lion walked off pleased later on he came across a zebra drinking at a water-hole the lion roared, 'Who is King of the Jungle?'

The zebra replied, 'Oh, you are, master.'

The lion walked off pleased further on he came across an elephant 'Who is King of the Jungle?' he roared with that the elephant threw the lion across a tree and jumped on him the lion scraped himself up off the ground and said, 'Okay, okay, there's no need to get mad just because you don't know the answer.'

4 Eight full stops are needed in this story. Retell it correctly.

A teenager started coming home in the early hours of Sunday morning his parents were worried and tried an experiment as he was driving back from a local disco, he was startled by a bell ringing in the glove-compartment opening it, he found an alarm-clock with a message tied to it the message read: 'This is the time we start worrying how about coming home?'

The following Saturday his parents were awakened by an alarm-clock hidden in the bedroom cupboard the note beside it said, 'Stop worrying and put on the coffee I will be home in ten minutes'

5 First write out the following passage with its five full stops in place.

In his early teens, a boy became a squire a knight might have several squires to follow him into battle they carried his shield and took charge of his horses if a squire did well in a war, he was knighted on the battlefield in time of peace, knighthood meant a night of prayer in a church it ended in the morning with the sword on the shoulder and the fastening of new golden spurs.

Then look at the nouns before and after the full stops which link the sentences. Underline the linking nouns in one colour, and the linking pronouns in another colour.

CAPITAL LETTERS

Capital letters are used for all proper nouns.
All names and words in titles have capitals.
Places, days of the week and months have capitals.
I is a capital letter when used by itself.
Talking must begin with a capital letter.
Addresses on envelopes have capital letters.
Letters beginning paragraphs have capitals.
Sentences *always* begin with a capital letter.

(a)   Write out the following, putting in all the capital letters and also the full stops

1   in the days of the romans, people knew of only three continents and divided the surface of the world between them in this proportion: europe, one third; africa, one quarter; asia one fifth; the rest of the world being water

2   mahommed died in the year 632 he had made the soldiers of allah promise that they would take the sword and the koran to the world in a few years they conquered palestine, egypt and libya, and had advanced across north africa to the shores of the atlantic

having moved up through spain, the arabs crossed the pyrenees they dreamed of conquering the world and changing it to the religion of islam, but in AD 732 charles martel, the king of the french, stopped them at poitiers although defeated in france the moslems settled themselves firmly in spain had it not been for the battle of poitiers, the history of europe might have been changed

about fifty years later, charlemagne, champion of rome and christianity fought on three fronts against the lombards, the moslems in spain and the saxons after many successful battles he became the emperor of the holy roman empire

(b)   Write out the following, putting in all capital letters.

1   I like hearing myself talk. it is one of my greatest pleasures. i often have long conversations all by myself, and i am so clever that sometimes i don't understand a single word of what i am saying.

2   An actor was offered £1000 a week to work on a new film.
'that's good pay', he said. 'what's it called?'
'*treasure island*,' replied the director. 'you will play long john silver. be on the set first thing on tuesday morning.'
'for that money,' said the actor, 'i don't mind starting monday.'
'not monday. on monday you're having your leg off.'

3   mad dogs and englishmen go out in the mid-day sun; the japanese don't care to, the chinese wouldn't dare to; hindus and argentines sleep firmly from twelve to one, but englishmen detest a — siesta.

4   'doctor, i get this feeling that nobody wants to speak to me.'
'next patient, please!'

5   john smith, 5 high street,
newtown, yorkshire

FULL STOP FOR ABBREVIATIONS

The full stop may be used for shortening one word. For example:
department — dept.   captain — capt.
or for shortening a group of words, for example:
Criminal Investigation Department — C.I.D.

(a)   Write the usual abbreviations for the following words.

1 centimetre
2 anonymous
3 for example
4 doctor

5 Bachelor of Arts
6 Victoria Cross
7 Hampshire
8 et cetera

(b)   Making use of your dictionary, write out in full what the following abbreviations stand for.

1 A.A.   7 M.D.   13 U.N.O.   19 N.S.P.C.C.
2 R.A.C.   8 R.N.   14 O.H.M.S.   20 Asst.
3 U.K.   9 R.A.F.   15 Y.M.C.A.   21 P.T.O.
4 B.B.C.   10 P.S.   16 Y.W.C.A.   22 R.S.V.P.
5 I.T.A.   11 Rev.   17 P.D.S.A.   23 G.M.T.
6 B.Sc.   12 abbr.   18 R.S.P.C.A.   24 W.H.O.

THE EXCLAMATION MARK

The exclamation mark is used when shouting.
For example: 'Help!'   'Stop, thief!'   'Halt!'   'Police!'

It is used when giving orders, for example:
'Come in!'   'Stand to attention!'   'Pass the ball!'

It is also used for the purpose of emphasis, or to give a sentence a special meaning that cannot be conveyed by a full stop. It should not, however, be used too often or its effect will be lost.

It may sometimes be used for effect after just one word, as in the following sign in a vet's waiting room:

Doctor will be with you shortly. Sit! Stay!

THE QUESTION MARK

> The question mark is placed at the end of a question. As it completes a sentence (in the same way as a full stop) the next word begins with a capital letter.

(a) The *Marie Celeste* was a mysterious sailing-ship which was found drifting on the ocean, with meals ready on the tables, but with not a soul on board the ship.

Write out the following questions about the ship, putting in all the question marks.

1 Where was the ship found
2 How did the crew escape
3 Did they in fact escape
4 Were there any survivors
5 Why was the ship abandoned

(b) Rewrite the following sentences so that they become questions, for example:

statement: It is time to go home.
question: Is it time to go home?

1 The last bus has gone.
2 We have money for the fare.
3 The journey will not take long.
4 We will have something to eat when we get home.
5 I wonder what time I should get up in the morning.

(c) The following stories have commas, but no full stops, question marks or exclamation marks. Write them out, putting in the missing marks, so that they make sense. Here is an example:

A: Do you believe in free speech?
B: I most certainly do!
A: Good. May I use your phone?

1 *Judge:*   What is your name, my man

Prisoner: My name, sir It's Bill Smith
Judge: Have you ever been up before me before
Prisoner: I don't know, sir What time do you get up

2 *Teacher:* Where is your pencil
Tommy: I ain't got one
Teacher: You must say 'haven't', not 'ain't' I haven't got my pencil, you haven't got a pencil, they haven't got pencils
Tommy: Hey What happened to all the pencils
Teacher: Don't be silly, Tommy If I had five apples in one hand, and six in the other, what would I have
Tommy: Big hands

3 *Teacher:* What is a cannibal
Elizabeth: Don't know, Miss
Teacher: Well, what would you be if you ate your mother and father
Elizabeth Please, Miss — an orphan

4 *Doctor:* Who's the patient
Nurse: A man who has had a golf ball knocked down his throat
Doctor: Who is the chap pacing up and down in the waiting-room
Nurse: Another golfer
Doctor: Well, what's he waiting for
Nurse: His ball back

THE COMMA

'COMMA LONG!'

The comma has three main purposes:

1 It shows the links between the different parts of a sentence.

2 It separates the different items in a list.

3 It marks off a name or description within a sentence.

(a) Write out the following stories, putting a comma after each item in a list.

1 *Station announcer:*
The train now arriving at platforms four five six and seven is coming in sideways!

2 *Rich customer on the phone:*
Now I want you to deliver me two dozen oysters not too large not too small not very old not tough and not sandy.
Fishmonger:
Certainly, madam. With or without pearls?

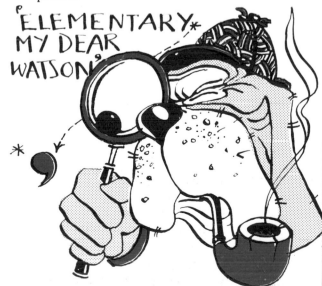

'ELEMENTARY MY DEAR WATSON'

The case of the missing comma

The following four uses of the comma should be noted:

1 To mark off a person's name from the rest of the sentence, for example:

'Come here, John, and be quick!'
'Where are you going now, John?'

2 To separate an extra description or name in the sentence, for example:

Miss Smith, the new English teacher, will be starting work tomorrow.
I hope to see the headmaster, Mr Roberts, at the meeting.

3 To separate a few words put in as 'a remark on the side', for example:

'I am confident that, no matter how long it takes, you will succeed.'
'You will, of course, get a year's guarantee with this radio.'

4 To mark off the end of the line of an address on an envelope or at the top of a letter, for example:

Mr John Smith,
  Flat 13,
    5 John Burns Street,
      Edinburgh,
        Scotland.

Mr J. Roberts, (Headmaster),
  New Comprehensive School,
    High Road,
      Manchester.

SPEECH MARKS

> **Speech marks are used to show that somebody has spoken, and they may be used as singles ('....') or as doubles ("....").**

Only the words *actually spoken* go *inside* the speech marks; all other words are outside. To show how this works, here is a conversation between the two people in the picture.

Voice on the phone:	Jimmy won't be coming to school today. He doesn't feel well.
Teacher:	That's all right. Who's speaking?
Voice:	My father, Miss.

There are three ways in which spoken words may be set out.

(1)   Spoken words at the *beginning* of the sentence, for example:

'Could you please tell me the time?' I asked.

(2)   Spoken words at the *end* of the sentence, for example:

I asked, 'Please could you tell me the time?'

Note that the word Please has a capital letter. This is because a capital letter *must* be used whenever a person *starts* to speak.

(3)   Spoken words *interrupted* in the sentence, for example:

'Could you please,' I asked, 'tell me the time?'

Note that the word *tell* does *not* have a capital letter. This is because it is not the first word spoken, and it does not start a new sentence.

'Could you please tell me the time?' is one sentence which has been interrupted.

Note also the use of the comma in the interrupted sentence. There is a comma after *please* to separate it from *I asked*, and there is a comma after *I asked* to separate the *unspoken* part of the sentence from the *spoken* part inside the speech marks.

(a)   Punctuate the following with speech marks, commas and full stops in the style of (1), (2) and (3) in the left-hand column.

(1) It is just two o'clock he replied
(2) He replied it is just two o'clock
(3) It is just two o'clock he replied so you had better get a move on

(b)   Punctuate the following story.

A man was walking in the park and found a penguin. He took it to a policeman and said I have found this penguin what should I do?

The policeman replied take him to the zoo.

The next day the policeman saw the man with the penguin and said I told you to take that penguin to the zoo!

I did that yesterday said the man. Today I am taking him to the movies.

SPEECH MARKS EXERCISES

> **When writing speech, always start a new line to show when there is a change of speaker.**

(a)   Write out the following story, putting in all the speech marks to make the sense clear.

A gorilla went into a pub, put £1.00 on the counter and asked for a pint of beer. The barman gave him a pint, 10p change and said, I hope you don't mind me staring at you, but we don't get many gorillas in here.

I'm not surprised, said the gorilla, at 90p for a pint of beer!

(b)   Write out the following passage from *Oliver Twist*, putting in all the speech marks as in the original book.

Hold your tongue, will you? said the jailer.

I'm an Englishman ain't I? rejoined the Artful Dodger. Where are my privileges?

You'll get your privileges soon enough, retorted the jailer, and pepper with 'em.

We'll see what the Secretary of State for Home Affairs has to say to the beaks if I don't, replied the Dodger.

Silence there! cried the clerk.

What is this? asked the magistrate.

A pick-pocketing case, your worship.

Has the boy ever been here before?

He ought to have been, many times, replied the jailer. I know him very well, your worship.

Now then, where are the witnesses? asked the clerk.

Ah! that's right, added Dodger. Where are they? I should like to see 'em.

Have you anything to ask this witness, boy? said the magistrate.

(c)   In your own words, write out a piece about a page long, carrying on the story of the Artful Dodger, asking questions of the witness, with the witness giving his answers. Use suitable verbs to describe the manner in which each character speaks.

(d)   Write out the following jokes so that they can be more easily understood. Put in all the speech marks and start a new line every time there is a change of speaker.

1   There's been an accident! they said. Your servant's cut in half; he's dead! Indeed! said Mr Jones, then please, send me the half that's got my keys.

2   This is a very good textbook said the shopkeeper. If you use it properly, I am sure it will do half your work for you. In that case, said the small boy, could I please buy two of them?

3   A farmer who did not like holidaymakers feeding his horse, pinned a notice to his fence: Please do not feed cakes and buns to the horse. Signed: The Owner. Shortly afterwards, another notice appeared below the first. It read: Please pay no attention to the above notice. Signed: The Horse.

4   The attendant at the boating lake was shouting. Come in number 91. No response. Come in number 91. Nothing! Are you in trouble number 16?

5   Doctor, I feel like a pair of curtains. Pull yourself together!

THE 'SHORTENING' APOSTROPHE

Another name for the 'raised comma' is the apostrophe. It enables you to leave out a letter (or letters) and put an apostrophe in the place where the letters used to be.

(a)   Write out in full the following shortened words.

1 I'm	9 we're
2 you're	10 they're
3 mustn't	11 wasn't
4 isn't	12 weren't
5 aren't	13 hasn't
6 who's	14 that's
7 you've	15 shouldn't
8 wouldn't	16 they've

(b)   Use the apostrophe to shorten:

1 did not	9 what is
2 should not	10 I have
3 you had	11 shall not
4 where is	12 I had
5 it is	13 you will
6 have not	14 how is
7 cannot	15 we have
8 we will	16 let us

(c)   Write out the following conversation between a mother and her daughter, putting in apostrophes.

'Whereve you been? Ive been looking everywhere.'
'Ive been down to the river to see if its wet.'
'Dont you be saucy to me! Say youre sorry!'

'O.K. Im sorry, I didnt mean it. Whats for supper?'
'Therell be no supper for you, my girl, until youve been upstairs and washed your hands.'

(b)   Here is another conversation between a mother and her son. Write it out, putting in all the punctuation and altering the words in red into shortened words with apostrophes.

Hurry up son or you will be late for school
   I shall not came the reply from the bedroom
   What is wrong asked his mother
   I do not like the teachers and I cannot stand the kids
   I will give you two good reasons why you should go
   What are they inquired the son
   One: you are thirty-five and two: you have just been made headmaster

THE 'OWNERSHIP' APOSTROPHE

Where does the apostrophe go to show that somebody owns something? Ask 'Who is the owner?' and put the apostrophe after the last letter of the owner's name.

A DOG'S COLLAR

If the owner is singular put the apostrophe at the end and add -s, for example:

This is the girl's bag.
That is Cass's dog.

If the owner is plural ending in -s, put the apostrophe *after* the -s, for example:

These are the girls' bags.

If the plural doesn't end in -s, for example: men, you still add the apostrophe after the owner's name and then add -s.

These are men's ties.

(a)   Put an apostrophe in these where necessary.

1 the miners lamps
2 a cats claws
3 ladies hairdresser
4 teachers lesson
5 Johns skateboard
6 the teams captain
7 the teams captains
8 Marys acquaintances
9 pop-groups manager
10 the hotels lounge

(b)   Rewrite the following so that an apostrophe is needed to show ownership.

1 the tail of the fox
2 the school of the boys
3 the fault of the girl
4 the Park of St James
5 the sister of the girl
6 pay for two weeks
7 the food at this café
8 headmaster of the school
9 the camp-site of the scouts
10 the report-sheets of the pupils

(c)   Write out numbers 1 and 2 below, complete with apostrophes; explain why number 3 is complete and does not need an apostrophe.

1 Loss of property is not the companys responsibility.
2 The two companies employees now work for different firms.
3 The two companies have been formed into one new company.

IT'S, HE'S, WHO'S

You use an apostrophe where two words have been brought together and shortened. Here are some examples:

IT'S – It's time for us to go home.
(It is time for us to go home.)
HE'S – He's not staying any longer.
(He is not staying any longer.)
WHO'S – This is my friend who's going to the party with us.
(This is my friend who is going to the party with us.)

Note: He's may also be used in place of *he has,* for example:
He's hooked the ball right out to the boundary.

It's may also be used in place of *it has,* for example:
It's been a lovely day.

Always test your spelling by checking whether you have put two words together.

If the word stands on its own, you don't need an apostrophe. For example:

ITS – The dog chases its own tail.
(note: not *it is* own tail)

WHOSE – This is my friend whose party we are going to.
(note: not my friend *who is* party)

(a)   Write out the following conversation, putting who's or whose inside the blank spaces.

'_____ being thrown out of "_____ WHO"?'
'I'm not sure; it's a chap _____ face is familiar, but _____ name I can't remember.'

(b) Write out the following, putting its, it's his, he's, whose and who's in the spaces.

1 Do you think _____ going to rain?
2 Oh dear, my umbrella has lost _____ handle!
3 I wish to see Mr Smith.
   Is this _____ office?
4 Yes, but _____ out at lunch.
5 _____ going to lay the table?
6 _____ job is it usually?
7 The cat looks after _____ kittens very well, because _____ a good mother.
8 I am pleased to say that _____ doing his best and _____ work shows signs of improvement.

YOUR AND YOU'RE, THEIRS AND THERE'S

① **YOU ARE**

② **YOU'RE A**

③ **YOU'RE**

① **THERE IS**

② **THERE'S**

③ **THERE'S**

YOUR }	both
THEIRS }	possessive

Here again, you only use an apostrophe if you are running two words together. For example:

YOU'RE – You're the next one to bat.
(You are the next one to bat.)

YOUR – Hurry up and get your pads.
(note: not *you are* pads)

THERE'S – There's no cake left over.
(There is no cake left over.)

THEIRS – These cakes are theirs.
(note: not cakes are *there is*)

Note: There's may also be used in place of *there has*. For example:

I hear there's been an accident.

Write out the following remarks, putting you're, your, there's and theirs inside the blank spaces.

1 'My child,' said the old lady. '_____ a good friend, and I will see that _____ kindness is rewarded.'

2 'My child,' said the old lady, '_____ one thing you must remember; always give to people what is rightly _____ .'

3 'My child,' said the old lady, '_____ coat does not do up to the neck. I shall knit you a scarf which _____ to wear when it's cold.'

4 'My child,' said the old lady, 'I know _____ fed up with me, so I shall be off and not get on _____ nerves any more.'

THERE, THEIR AND THEY'RE

place:
standing over there

possessive:
their brushes and paints

abbreviation:
meaning 'they are'

Be careful not to confuse these three words which sound the same, but mean different things, so are spelt in different ways.

(a)   Write out the following sentences, putting there, their and they're inside the blank spaces. Look at the examples above first.

1 'Go over _____ where I can see you.'
2 '_____ maths books are here.'
3 '_____ collecting up all the maths books.'
4 'I don't know what I've done with _____ pens.'
5 'If they don't hurry up _____ not going to be in time for the film.'

(b)   Here are some variations. Rewrite the following, putting their, there, there's, they're, they've and theirs inside the blank spaces.

1 'In my opinion, _____ no use having an argument about the matter.'
2 'They think _____ no chance of winning _____ field-event.'

3 'Your coat is over _____ on the second hanger.'
4 'I think that these coats are _____.'
5 '_____ another question you have to answer.'
6 '_____ no business like show business.'
7 'Give them back what's _____ as they have a right to _____ own property.'
8 'The house I'm looking for is over _____.'
9 'I don't think _____ any right to claim what isn't _____.'
10 '_____ you are; _____ right after all!'
11 '_____ got ten minutes left to finish the examination.'
12 'What's yours is yours and what's _____ must be _____.'
13 'I think _____ doing _____ best, but it's not very good.'
14 '_____ a tavern in the town, in the town, and _____ my true love sits her down.'
15 'We will go to the box-office to see if _____ a single seat left, but _____ not much hope.'

WHERE, WEAR, WERE AND WE'RE

verb: to wear your clothes

verb: we were there

abbreviation:
short for we are

place: where are you?

These words all sound similar, but each has a different meaning and spelling. Look at the examples above.

(a) Write out the following sentences, putting where, wear, were and we're in the blank spaces.

1 'Come over here _____ I can see you!'
2 'Your exercise-books _____ here a minute ago.'
3 '_____ are your pencils?'
4 '_____ going to the park to hear the band playing.'
5 'You _____ told to _____ your school tie!'
6 'Is this the place _____ _____ supposed to meet?'

(b) Write out the following sentences, putting where, were, wear, we're and where's in the spaces.

1 'Hello, Mary, _____ have you been hiding yourself?'
2 'I shall _____ my blue dress for the party tonight.
   What kind of dress _____ you going to _____ ?'

3 'Mum! _____ my blue dress?'
4 'I bet my sister's taken it. _____ going to have a row about this.'

(c) Write out the following passage, putting these words inside the blank spaces, using each word once only: where, wear, were, we're, weir, where's, wearing, wears and wore.

One day we went for a walk by the river.
   '_____ that noise coming from?' I asked my friend.
   'From the _____ round the bend of the river,' she said.
   As it was warm, we _____ _____ cool clothes. My friend _____ a purple tee-shirt, a colour she often _____ . I dislike the colour and _____ often arguing about it, but she says she will _____ what she likes _____ she pleases.

HERE AND HERE'S, HEAR AND HEARS

abbreviation:
short for 'here is'

verb: I can hear you

he hears
me speak

place: right here

Look at the examples above.

(a)   Write out the following, putting here, hear, hears and here's inside the blank spaces.

1 'Come over _____ where I can see what you are doing!'
2 'Your exercise-books are _____ .'
3 'Louder, please, I can't _____ you.'
4 '_____ your exercise-book.'
5 The soldier _____ the order and carries out his duties.

(b)   Rewrite the following, putting one of these words in the blank spaces.

here   here's   hears   hear
heard   hair   herd

1 'Hello, Mary, I _____ you've been picked for the team to play _____ next Saturday.'
2 'I have _____ that you are not in the netball team.'

3 At the farm, I helped milk a _____ of Jersey cows.
4 '_____ a comb; now go and comb your untidy _____ !'
5 When he _____ the whistle, the sheep-dog follows him.

(c)   Write out the following passage, putting these words in the spaces, using each word once only.

here's   heard   hearing   hair
hare   hares   herd

At the pet-shop, I asked about the grey _____ in the window.
'_____ a leaflet,' said Mr Jones. 'It tells you all about the animal; how to brush its _____ and look after its big ears. Don't forget that its _____ is very important to it, because in the wild, a _____ of _____ rely on what is _____ more than on what is seen.'

'MYSTERY' WORDS

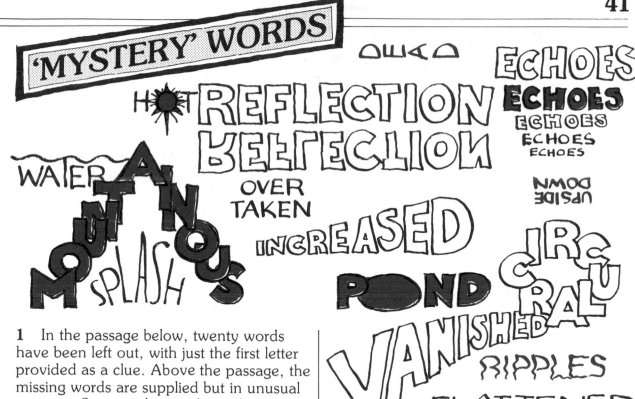

1   In the passage below, twenty words have been left out, with just the first letter provided as a clue. Above the passage, the missing words are supplied but in unusual patterns. Sort out the words, and as you write out the passage, place the words in the correct spaces, using each word once only. One more thing: the punctuation has also been left out. When you write out the passage, supply the punctuation needed, and put capital letters where necessary.

The sad story of Henry

One h…. day henry went for a walk into the country he passed a p…. saw his r…. in the w…. and threw in a stone with a great s…. he i…. his pace and headed for m….country giving a b…. glance at the c…. r…. as they slowly v…. from the surface of the pond.

   Upon reaching the mountains he gave a shout hello which set up loud e…. it must have been raining because the ground was wet and its surface very s…. because of this he fell down a steep s…. landing heavily u…. a h…. boulder slid down and f…. him he was d…. fates messenger had o…. him and nothing remained for him but the u….

2   Once you have filled in the gaps, write out a list of the words you have used, in the same order as they appear in the story. Against each word write out its part of speech (noun, verb, adjective, adverb) according to the way in which the word has been used. The first word is done for you:

hot – adjective

EITHER AND NEITHER EACH AND ANYONE

As shown above, the word *or* follows *either* and the word *nor* follows *neither*.

(a)   Write out the following, filling in the two blank spaces.

1 You *must* answer question A but may choose _____ B _____ C.
2 'Do you stir your tea with your left hand or your right hand?'
   '_____ left _____ right; I use a spoon!'

Either and *neither* can also be used in the plural with a *plural* verb.

(b)   Write out the following, putting a *plural* verb in each space.

1 Neither we nor they _____ going out.
2 Either the English or the French athletes _____ been chosen to begin.
3 Neither these nor those _____ fresh.

But note:
Neither Jane nor Anne drinks coffee.
The verb is singular even though two people are mentioned, because the sentence is talking about what each of them does *singly*. The clue to the verb is to see whether the nouns *on their own* are singular or plural.

The following six words are *always* used with a singular verb, as you can tell from the 'one' or 'body' included in the word.

each   anyone   anybody
nobody   everyone   everybody

(c)   Write out the following sentences, putting suitable *singular* verbs inside the blank spaces.

1 Each of us _____ to do his or her best in the examination.
2 Everyone in this country _____ compelled to attend some kind of school.
3 When it comes to _____ put in goal, anybody may be chosen.
4 Is there anyone here who can _____ a good game of tennis?
5 Nobody _____ to play the part of the wicked villain in the play.
6 Everybody _____ his or her personal belongings in the lockers provided.
7 Neither John nor Jim _____ much chance of being in the cricket team.
8 Either she plays a solo on the piano or you _____ her in a duet.

DOUBLE NEGATIVE

A negative is a word which gives the meaning of *no* or *not*. If you put *two* negatives into one sentence, the second will cancel the first, and the meaning of *no* or *not* will be lost.

The remark 'Nobody tells me nothing' contains a double negative, and should be written with only *one* negative, for example:
'Nobody tells me anything,' or 'Nothing ever reaches me.' Otherwise it means, 'Everybody tells me something.'

Rewrite the following sentences, taking out one of the negatives, so that the sentence means what the writer intended.

1 'I shan't tell no one what you did yesterday.'
2 'I've not got no more money to lend you for sweets.'
3 'She hasn't done nothing she needs to be ashamed of.'
4 'He has not spoken to neither of them for days.'
5 'There will not never be enough room in this town for Mr Not and Mr Never.'

DOUBLE COMPARATIVE DOUBLE SUPERLATIVE

A double comparative is as confusing as taking two photographs on one negative. You don't need to say the same thing twice over.

You may not say that one thing is *more better* than another, or that one thing is the *most best* out of all the other things.

Correct the following sentences.

1 The Eiffel Tower is more taller than Blackpool Tower.
2 It is well known that anglers tell the most tallest tales.
3 My sister is more cleverer than anyone in her class.
4 My sister is the most cleverest girl in her class at school.
5 He is the most worst behaved boy I have ever come across.

WRITE AND RIGHT

WRITE THESE WORDS..

'Right, my lad! You have the right to remain silent, but I will write down anything you say, and it may be used as evidence in court.'

(a) Write out the following, putting write or right inside the blank spaces.

1 'I wish I knew the _____ way to _____ an official letter of complaint to the Housing Department.'

2 'I am a self-made man, and you may _____ down the secret of success. It is not only being in the _____ place at the _____ time but also being in the _____ frame of mind.'

3 I have to _____ out a hundred times: 'It is not _____ to _____ the word _____ without the letter W.'

4 'Turn _____ at the traffic-lights, take the second turning on the _____ and go _____ ahead for the motorway.'

5 *Advertisement:* 'Are you illiterate? _____ to address below for free help. Only for _____-handed illiterates.'

WHETHER AND WEATHER

EMERGENCY SERVICE WEATHER FORECAST

BAD WEATHER

'Oh dear! I foresee bad weather, whether it's forecast or not.'

YES NO

whether

(b) Look at the examples above. Then write out the following, putting whether or weather in the spaces.

1 'I don't know _____ the _____ will be warm enough for swimming.'

2 'Stop making excuses for being late! I am not interested in _____ you could not get up because of the cold _____, or _____ or not you remembered to set your alarm-clock.'

3 'This is a report from the Met. Office. Today will be warm and dry, _____ permitting. But the forecaster has not come in this morning, so there will be no _____ tomorrow! Terribly sorry!'

CAN AND MAY

Can and may are often confused. Can is *capable* of doing what it wishes to do; may has first of all to obtain *permission*.

Write out the following, putting can or may inside the blank spaces.

1   I _____ take photographs inside the theatre, but the rules state that nobody _____ do so.

2   If you cannot answer question number 1, you _____ attempt 2 instead. You _____ leave the room when you wish, but you must hand in your papers at the desk.

3   '_____ I have a chocolate biscuit?'
'Now you know that is not the right way to ask.'
'_____ I have a chocolate biscuit?'
'What word have you left out?'
'_____ I *please* have a chocolate biscuit?'
'No! It's too near tea-time.'

e.g. and i.e.

e.g. This is an abbreviation of two Latin words, *exempli gratia* meaning 'for example' or 'for instance'.

We have several records of old 'pop' groups, *e.g.* The Beatles and The Shadows.

i.e. This is an abbreviation of two Latin words *id est* meaning 'that is to say' or 'an explanation is now given'.

You *can* leave the room, i.e. You are capable of leaving, but you did not ask if you had permission to leave the room.

MAY AND MIGHT

May and might are similar in meaning:
may is used when there is a fair possibility
that something will happen;
might is used when there is less possibility
that it will happen.
For example:
She *may* get the first prize.
(This means it is quite possible)
She *might* get the first prize.
(This means there is a possibility but it is
not very likely)

(a)   Write out the following, choosing may
or might .

1   Although the boxer is inexperienced he
_____ beat his tough opponent.

2   I have a lot of work to do and _____
arrive later for the party. I will probably

stay to the end but I _____ have to leave
a little early.

Might is also used as the past tense of may.
For example:

Present tense 'May I leave the table?' 'Yes
you may, if you have finished.'

Past tense The boy asked whether he
might leave the table. His mother said that
he might do so if he had finished.

FORMER AND LATTER

THE FORMER IS THE FIRST OF TWO

THE LATTER IS THE SECOND OF TWO

You have won a prize of either a trip to
America or £1000. Which would you
choose, the former or the latter? Write out
your answer, using the words former and
latter .

EMPLOYER AND EMPLOYEE

Dear Sir,
        Tom was my employee for two
weeks. Any employer who gets Tom to
work for him will be very lucky.
                        Yours faithfully,
                        John Smith

In your own words, explain why Tom
would be unwise to show the above letter
to a prospective employer.

TO, TOO AND TWO

To fits in the small gaps between words: *to* go *to* town.

Too is long and emphatic: *too* large or *too* low. It also means *as well*.

Two is the *number 2*.

(a)   Write out the following sentences, putting to, too or two inside the blank spaces.

1   I am going _____ see Manchester United on Saturday.
2   I want _____ see that match; may I come _____ ?
3   Yes, if you want _____ I'll get _____ tickets.

4   They won their last _____ games by _____ clear goals.
5   Sunderland is a good team _____ but they will have _____ improve a good deal if they hope _____ beat United.
6   Never! Sunderland is much _____ good a team for them.
7   I want you to push this button after I have counted 'one, _____ ', and then I want you to push this one _____ .
8   Are you ready, runners? One _____ get ready; _____ _____ get steady; three to be off!

(b)   Write out the following passage, putting to , too or two inside the blank spaces.

'Why do you have _____ attend _____ meetings in one evening? I want _____ go out _____, and I can't find a baby-sitter. It's _____ bad of you _____ make such awkward arrangements. I have only _____ evenings left before I have _____ go _____ work on the night-shift.'

NO, KNOW AND NOW

NO: I've no idea
KNOW: To know the answer
NOW: Now is the time

Look at the examples above. Then write out the following, putting no , know or now inside the spaces.

1   _____ person is allowed in that room, _____ not even you!
2   I don't _____ how you expected me to _____ that fact, _____ or any other time.
3   There is a notice on the door which says '_____ Entry'. You do _____ how to read, don't you?
4   _____ that you mention it, I did see the notice, but I ignored it. Anyway, what room can I use _____ ?
5   I don't _____; it's up to you _____ to make inquiries.

OFF AND OF

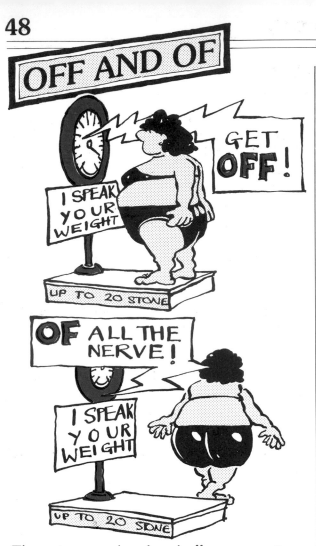

These two words, of and off, mean quite different things.

To get your spelling right, think how you say the word:

if it sounds like 'ov' you spell it of; if it has a double 'f' sound you spell it off.

Write out the following sentences, putting of or off in the spaces.

1   Keep _____ the grass as it is out _____ bounds.

2   '_____ with her head!' yelled the Red Queen.

3   'Kindly take your big foot _____ my poor toe!'

4   '_____ all my friends, I like your company best _____ all.'

5   'Don't turn _____ the tap; I need another pail _____ water.'

6   '_____ course you are welcome; please take _____ your coat.'

7   'Get out _____ the penalty-area; you are _____ -side.'

8   'Well, _____ course, if you are going to take that attitude, I shall be _____ and keep out _____ your way in future.'

9   'I should not have eaten all _____ that cake; it's made me feel quite _____ -colour.'

10   The word _____ spelt with one 'f' sounds as though it was 'ov'; the word spelt with two letters 'f' sounds like '_____'. Never use _____ and _____ together; it is incorrect.

should have   would have   must have
could have   might have   may have

In writing speech, we sometimes put should've (short for should have). It is possible to make a mistake and write should of (as the 'v' sound is similar) but the word of must never follow the words shown on the cover of the book below.

Here are some examples of correct uses:

I should have known better than that.
You could have told me earlier.
I would have taken it for you.
I might have known not to wait.
I must have left my keys at home.
I may have to take the last train.

TEACH AND LEARN LEND AND BORROW

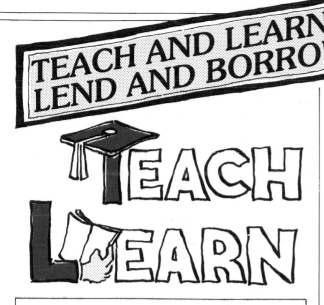

TEACH
LEARN

> A teacher *gives out* knowledge.
> A learner *takes in* knowledge.

LEND
BORROW

> A lender *hands out* articles.
> A borrower *takes in* articles.

(a)   Write out the following, putting teach, learn, lend or borrow inside the blank spaces.

1   My big brother has promised to _____ me how to swim.

2   If you want to play tennis, Mary will be pleased to _____ you.

3   I would like to _____ how to swim the crawl-stroke.

4   We will _____ how to play, at the tennis-club.

5   My pencil's broken; would you mind if I _____ yours?

6   I haven't a pencil but I can _____ you a pen; let me have it back.

7   I'm not going to _____ you anything else in future.

8   You always forget your gear and _____ mine.

9   Please _____ it to me and I won't _____ anything else.

10   Don't _____ from friends who may be unwilling to _____ .

(b)   Rewrite the following, putting one of these words in the spaces:

borrow   lending   borrowing
learnt   taught   borrowed   teach
loan   lent   lend

1   My father _____ me not to _____ money to others.

2   I am not _____ any more money from you.

3   I will _____ a book from the _____-library.

4   I once _____ a lot from old examination-papers.

5   I am going to _____ you a lesson that a _____ must be repaid.

6   When you have _____ money you are that much poorer.

7   When you have _____ money you are that much richer.

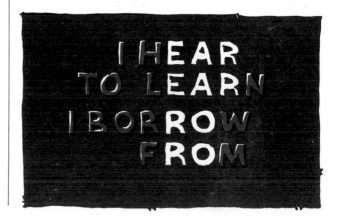

I HEAR TO LEARN
I BORROW FROM

THE CONJUNCTION

The conjunction (also known as the *joining word*) joins two or more phrases to make one complete sentence.

Sometimes the conjunction joins two parts which could be separate complete sentences, for example:

John walked along the street and turned round the corner.
John walked along the street. He turned round the corner.

These two sentences each have their own verbs.
The first one has the verb *walked* and the second one has *turned*.

Sometimes the conjunction joins two parts *only one of which* is a complete sentence, for example:

John walked along the street and round the corner.

'round the corner' has no verb and so is not a sentence.

The conjunction and is the most commonly used, but it is a 'weak' join, and there are

many words which make a 'stronger' and more suitable join.

Write out the following sentences, replacing *and* with a more suitable conjunction chosen from the 'notice-board' in the drawing on the next page.

1 Mary was chosen for the team *and* she is a very good player.
2 He wanted to play centre-forward *and* he has been put in goal.
3 We are going out for a long walk *and* it looks like rain.
4 This is a good shop *and* you can buy delicious chocolates.
5 The actors bowed to the audience *and* the play ended.

Three short sentences may be joined to form one complete sentence by using *two* conjunctions, for example:

(1) She came home late at night.
(2) She was very tired.
(3) She went straight to bed.

She came home late at night *and* went straight to bed *because* she was very tired.

Conjunctions give your writing better style, by linking several actions within one sentence.

CHOOSING THE CONJUNCTION

'I sentence you to hard labour in choosing conjunctions.'

WHILE YET FOR WHEN UNTIL OR BEFORE THAT AFTER NOR BUT AS ALTHOUGH THAN BECAUSE SINCE THOUGH UNLESS WHERE HOW WHETHER IF

(a)   Write out the following stories, choosing suitable conjunctions from the above notice-board to put into the blank spaces.

1   Two snakes were moving through the jungle _____ one snake asked the other whether they were poisonous and on being asked why, replied it was _____ he had just bitten his lip.

2   The spy asked if he could sing a song _____ the firing-squad shot him and _____ being told he could, he started to sing 'Ten thousand green bottles!'

3   'Auntie, did you feel any pain _____ you fell out of the willow-tree? I would like to know _____ you would be kind enough to do it again _____ my friend here wasn't looking.'

4   Once a farmer had a large hay field _____ his son was not happy in the country so moved to the town to look for a job, _____ the only job he could get was shining shoes. Now the farmer makes hay _____ the son shines.

(b)   Use different conjunctions to combine the following four short sentences into one long sentence.

The secondary school sports were held on the local playing fields. No records were broken. Conditions on the field were very poor. There had been heavy rain overnight.

(c)   A conjunction may be used at the beginning of a sentence as well as in the middle, for example:

She came home late at night.
She felt very tired.

When she came home late at night, she felt very tired.

Join the following sentences by using a conjunction at the beginning.

1   _____ you like it or not, you must go and visit grandmother.
2   _____ I have written twice, she has not bothered to reply.
3   _____ the audience had settled, the orchestra began to play.

THE WRONG USE OF 'THEN' AND 'SO'

GET RID OF
THE PESTS
THEN & SO

Then means 'the very next thing to happen'.

So means 'because of something that has just happened'.

All too often they are used to take the place of other correct and more suitable conjunctions. Then and so can become a menace to your writing if they are over-used.

In the following passage, the words *then* and *so* have been deliberately over-used. Write out the passage, replacing then and so with more imaginative words, and make any other alterations to sentences you think would improve the passage.

My Uncle George took me on a visit to London last Saturday so we went on the underground train to Baker Street Station then it was a short walk to Madame Tussaud's Museum. I wanted to see the Chamber of Horrors, so we went to see all the dreadful murderers, then we went into the planetarium which was next door, so then we were amazed at the views of the night sky.

So then after lunch we went for a walk by the side of the River Thames so as to have a look at the Houses of Parliament, then visit Westminster Abbey so we could see the famous tombs and then walk round the outside. So then after tea at the Royalty Restaurant, we then took a taxi to Victoria Station so we could go home by train.

So when we got home we told Mum and Dad where we had been. Then we had supper and then after we had finished I went to bed, and so that was the end of my interesting day.

CONJUNCTIONS TO DO WITH TIME

as	when	till
before	since	while
after	until	whenever

(a)   Put words from the above list inside the blank spaces of the following sentences, using each word once only.

1   She watched the car _____ it disappeared from view.

2   I shall wait patiently _____ I see a chance to score.

3   _____ she left the shop, she has been out of work.

4   He sleeps and takes it easy _____ I go out to work.

5   They will think carefully _____ they make their move.

6   _____ I made a move, the guard-dog growled menacingly.

7   I am ready to go _____ you wish to go home.

8   I shall come round to your house _____ you like.

9   _____ she had finished her work she went to see a film.

'SPECIAL MEANING' CONJUNCTIONS

but	although	provided
unless	as	whether
if	because	where

(b)   Put words from the above list inside the blank spaces of the following sentences, using each word once only.

1   She will not come to the party _____ she gets an invitation.

2   _____ it grew colder, they put on their coats and scarves.

3   _____ we like playing hockey, we prefer to play netball.

4   I cannot help being nervous _____ of the exams tomorrow.

5   I will take your place in the team _____ you don't feel well.

6   She would like to be chosen _____ she knows she is unsuitable.

7   Mary can join the team _____ she attends all the practice games.

8   The captain does not know _____ to bat or field.

9   The team members will meet _____ the meeting was held last time.

RELATIVE PRONOUNS WHO AND WHICH

I SUPPORT MY MOTHER WHO IS BLIND

AND MY DOG WHICH IS LAME

WHO IS FOR PEOPLE

WHICH IS FOR ANIMALS & THINGS

Look at the examples above.
Who and which are called *relative pronouns,* because they join or relate two phrases, by taking the place of a noun.

Without a relative pronoun:
I support my mother.
My mother is blind.

With a relative pronoun:
I support my mother who is blind.

'Who' takes the place of the repeated noun, and joins the two sentences in one.

Now join each of these pairs of sentences into one sentence by using who for people, which for animals and things. You will

sometimes have to change the order of phrases so that the new sentence makes sense.

1 In the hall I found a £1 note.
  I handed it in to the secretary.
2 The attendant saved the child.
  She had fallen in the deep-end.
3 John is captain of the team.
  He received the silver cup.
4 Dad has bought a cocker-spaniel.
  It has to have a daily walk.
5 My friends stayed until 10 p.m.
  They had only come for tea!
6 The pen was under a desk.
  It had rolled along the floor.
7 The teacher was ready for her pupils.
  They arrived on time.

WHO AND WHOM

The man who hit me   **The man whom I hit**

Whom is another relative pronoun. You don't hear it very often, because a lot of people forget to use it. But here are some examples of its correct use:
The man whom I hit.
The girls whom I saw.

Compare them with these examples:
The man who hit me.
The girls who saw me.

Can you see the difference? In the first examples, the action is being done *to* the man and the girls; we say they are the *object* of the verb.

In the second examples, it is the other way round; the man and the girls are doing the actions, and we say they are the *subject* of the verb.

One way to remember the difference between who and whom is that if you would use *him* or *them* for the pronoun, then whom is correct. For example:
The man whom I hit.
I hit him.
but
The man who hit me.
He hit me.

Now try this exercise, filling in who or whom in the right places.

1 The man _____ hit me broke his wrist.
2 The man _____ I hit fell downstairs.
3 The girls _____ saw me won the cup.
4 The girls _____ you saw left the country.
5 The sister _____ I like best climbs trees.
6 The brother _____ we know least well can't cook.

Now try and explain the difference between who and whom to someone who doesn't understand it.

WHOSE

Whose is the _possessive_ relative pronoun; it indicates ownership on the part of the noun. Whose is used for people and things.

Here is an example:
The hunter followed the tigers.
Their tracks could clearly be seen.
(_their_ indicates possession)

This can be written as one sentence:
The hunter followed the tigers whose tracks could clearly be seen.

Revision: Write out the following sentences, putting who , whose or whom inside the blank spaces.

1 Litter-louts don't care _____ they put to inconvenience.
2 We found some football shirts and wondered _____ they were.
3 He gave me the cookery-book and told me to find out _____ owned it.
4 The Head is pleased with the new teacher _____ she has just engaged.
5 The Head is pleased with the new teacher _____ started last week.
6 The police are not certain _____ to place under arrest.
7 The referee has to decide _____ (if anybody) was off-side.
8 The referee has to decide _____ free-kick it is this time.
9 Two cannibals fighting raises the question, _____ will eat _____ ?
10 They've lighted their fires and made water hot;
I wonder just _____ will end up in _____ pot!

THE PLACING OF RELATIVE PRONOUNS

The relative pronoun must be placed _as close as possible_ to the word it stands for.

If the relative pronoun is not placed close to the word it stands for, the sentence may be hard to understand, or may give quite the wrong meaning.

Wrong example: The _bride_ was given away by her father, _who_ wore a dress of white satin.

CORRECTION: The _bride, who_ wore a dress of white satin, was given away by her father.

Rewrite the following correctly:
1 The antique armchair cost £1000, on which he carefully sat down.
2 The young girl married a soldier who was the Major's daughter.
3 The owner of the pet shop kept a parrot who had a long beard.
4 Children accompanied by adults who are under three years of age will be admitted free of charge.

LETTER WRITING

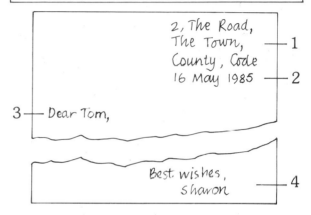

> Mr Tom James,
> 63, New Road,
> Duncanstown,
> Lanarkshire, LS5 6J

Letters may be roughly divided into two kinds: business and personal.

Address your envelope like this for *business* or *personal* letters.

3 — Personnel Manager,
Ever-running Shoes,
Factory Road,
Clee thorpes
4 — Dear Sir/Madam,

2, The Road, — 1
The Town,
County, Code
16 May 1985 — 2

Yours faithfully, — 5
Sharon Smith

2, The Road, — 1
The Town,
County, Code
16 May 1985 — 2

3 — Dear Tom,

Best wishes, — 4
Sharon

The business letter

Points to remember:

1 Your own address, top right-hand corner

2 The date, below the address

3 The business address you are writing to

4 If you don't know the exact name to use, write Sir, Madam or Sir/Madam

5 If you have addressed the person by name, end with Yours sincerely, but if you have only used their title, end with Yours faithfully.

Now try writing these business letters:

(a) to an employer, asking for a job

(b) to a theatre, asking to book tickets

(c) to a company, complaining of faulty goods

The personal letter

Points to remember:

1 Your own address, top right-hand corner

2 Date, just below

3 Either use the Christian name, if you know the person well, or Mr, Mrs, Miss or Ms if you only know them by surname.

4 The easiest endings to use are Best wishes, Yours or Love from, according to how well you know the person.

Now try writing these personal letters:

(a) to a relative, thanking her for a present

(b) to a friend, thanking him for a day out

(c) to a friend, apologising for forgetting her birthday

PARAGRAPHS

CHANGE OF PERSON

> **When a new person is introduced, a new paragraph is required.**

In the year 1100, while hunting in the New Forest, William II was killed by an arrow. His body, still dripping with blood, was carried on a farm wagon to Winchester for burial. An accident? Or was it murder?

One man stood to gain by William's death. This was his younger brother Henry, who was also hunting in the forest at the time. He galloped instantly to Winchester to take possession of the royal treasure which was kept there, and then on to London to be crowned king.

CHANGE OF SPEAKER

> **When one person has stopped speaking, a new paragraph is required to make it quite clear that a different person is replying.**

'Four years ago, the accused was arrested on a similar charge and released through lack of evidence. In my opinion…'

'I object, your Honour!' interrupted the barrister.

'On what grounds, counsel for the defence?'

'What my learned friend has mentioned has no bearing on the present case and is not admissible as evidence.'

'I agree; objection sustained. The jury will disregard the last remark of the counsel for the prosecution!'

'But your Honour, my learned friend didn't give me a chance to finish my sentence and explain. In my opinion…'

'Overruled!'

PARAGRAPHS

CHANGE OF PLACE

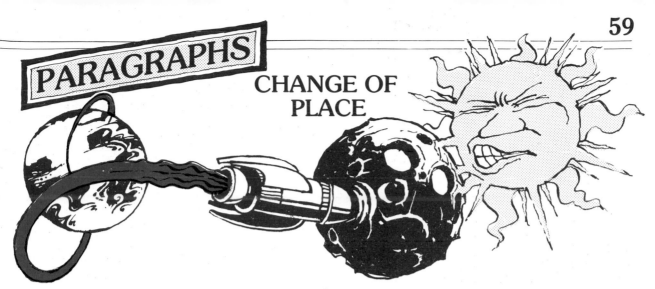

> **For a change of place make space for a change.**

For the first few days our space rocket kept up a steady speed of about 20,000 miles an hour. But as we got close to the moon, the retro-rockets were switched on to slow us down and we made a smooth landing.

We stared with amazement at the strange world on which we stood. It was absolutely bare of grass, trees and water, and seemed to consist only of grey dust and rocks with huge craters everywhere. Far, very far away, glowed our golden planet, looking like an enormous moon.

CHANGE OR PASSING OF TIME

> **When it's change of *time,* it is time for a *change.***

You may have heard of the expression 'being in the limelight'. This goes back to the days when a gas made from lime was burnt to make a bright spotlight on the stage. An actor standing in the limelight stood out among his fellow actors.

About sixty years later, electricity was introduced into the theatre, putting an end to the old limelight. When we now go to the theatre or watch plays and shows on the television, we can see a star performer picked out in a bright electric spotlight. This is both brighter and safer than the old limelight, but the performer is still 'in the limelight'.

THE FINAL PARAGRAPH

There are many ways of ending a story, but the important thing is that the *last paragraph must seem to be final;* the reader has to feel that one more paragraph would spoil the effect. The following brief tale shows the *finality* of the last paragraph.

Alexander the Great one day wandered to the Gates of Paradise. He knocked on the gates and was asked his name. He said he was Alexander, Conqueror of the World, but the answer came that he could not enter as they had never heard of him.

He asked for something to prove that he had reached the heavenly gates, and a small piece of a human skull was thrown to him with the words '*Take this and see how much it weighs!*' He took it to his generals who looked at it with contempt. They brought a pair of scales and, placing the bone in one pan, put a pile of gold coins in the other; the little bone outweighed the gold.

Alexander then put on the scales his helmet made of pure silver and his famous sword with emeralds and rubies in the hilt, but to no effect. Finally, he added his great gold crown studded with pearls and diamonds, but all the gold, silver and jewels flew upwards like feathers.

A wise and holy man was sent for. He thought for a moment, then took a few grains of dust from the earth and sprinkled them on the bone. Up flew the scale with the bone and down crashed the gold, the sword, the helmet and the crown of the man who ruled the world.

'*That bone,*' said the Wise Man, '*came from the socket which goes round the eye, and nothing will satisfy the human eye until it is covered by the dust of the grave.*'

THE 'SUMMING UP' PARAGRAPH

Near the end of a court case, the court will go over the main points of the evidence. In a composition containing different points of view, the last paragraph can *sum up* by very briefly stating the main points, and making clear your personal opinion.